PRAISE FOR JENNIFER MACBAIN-STEPHENS

A straightforward urgency accompanies the timely profundity and deft perceptiveness of the poems in *The Messenger Is Already Dead*, anchored in experiences of violence against the female body. Jennifer MacBain-Stephens writes plainly, "You cannot kill me / I am already dead," flaunting immortality as a reflection of agency too difficult and dangerous to achieve by quotidian means. One female speaker proudly chooses to "plunge from the highest masthead" to achieve the invulnerable state of death; another, burned alive, "dips her toe into the afterlife, and she is glowing." Still other poems interrogate the films of Man Ray—whose work inspired the Black Dahlia's killer—and examine the mixed-media work of visual artist Jenny Holzer, whose "prophetic/ billboards above strip clubs" carry messages such as, "Abuse of power comes as no surprise." Immersing oneself in this book, even the most tenacious reader will be confronted with the possibility of losing her grip on the narrative threads we spin—for whom?—about what and who keeps us safe in these bodies, in this world.
 —Fox Frazier-Foley

Clown Machine is a delicious spectacle in which we should all indulge. Reading this collection immediately made me think of the current state of political affairs in this country: the circus of it all…MacBain-Stephens presents us a spectacular circus of moving pieces, and a look at the tenuous sideshow inside of us that begs to be seen. It's as if the author has a portal into all of our interior empty nooks that long for more than we've got, or want more than we should.
 —Amy Strauss-Friedman

Clearly, MacBain-Stephens understands the texture of words, understands the need to feel them on teeth and tongue…Her language is that of the synapse, firing off psychedelic sparks that invite, intrigue, and infiltrate.
 —Dianne Borsenik

ACKNOWLEDGMENTS AND NOTES

Some of these poems first appeared in FLAPPERHOUSE, Bareknuckle Poet: Journal of Letters, Quailbell Magazine, The Poetry Storehouse, Thirteen Myna Birds, seinundwerden, Jet Fuel Review, Uppagus, Otoliths, Pith, E*ratio Literary Journal, Underground Books: The Kitchen Poet, The Birds we Piled Loosely, the weirderary, Inter/rupture Poor Claudia, Rogue Agent, fog machine, Lime Hawk, Sea Foam Magazine, Riding Light Review, and Pretty Owl Poetry.

Some of the Joan of Arc poems were collected in a chapbook (*Jeanne: Poems about Revenge, Ants and Light*) which was one of the winners of the Be About it Press chapbook contest. Thanks to Alexandra Naughton.

The poem "Land Surveyor" was remixed into a poem/movie by Marc Neys, aka "Swoon," with audio recorded by John Vickery. This video can be found at The Poetry Storehouse and at Vimeo.

Some text in italics in the Jenny Holzer poems are quotation from the artist herself, from the book *Jenny Holzer* - Phaidon Publishing (1998).

THE MESSENGER IS ALREADY DEAD

ALSO BY JENNIFER MACBAIN-STEPHENS

Clown Machine

Your Best Asset is a White Lace Dress

xx poems

Clotheshorse

Every Her Dies

Backyard Poems

Jeanne

The Visitant

JENNIFER MACBAIN STEPHENS

THE MESSENGER IS ALREADY DEAD

Stalking Horse Press
Santa Fe, New Mexico

THE MESSENGER IS ALREADY DEAD
Copyright © 2016 by Jennifer MacBain-Stephens
ISBN: 978-0-9984339-2-9
Library of Congress Control Number: 2016961147

First paperback edition published by Stalking Horse Press, March 2017

All rights reserved. Except for brief passages quoted for review or academic purposes, no part of this book may be reproduced, stored in a retrieval system, or transmitted by any means without the written permission of the author and publisher. Published in the United States by Stalking Horse Press.

The characters and events in this book are fictitious or used fictitiosly. Any similarity to real persons, living or dead, is coincidental and not intended by the author.

www.stalkinghorsepress.com

Design by James Reich

Stalking Horse Press
Santa Fe, New Mexico

Stalking Horse Press requests that authors designate a nonprofit, charitable, or humanitarian organization to receive a portion of revenue from the sales of each title. Jennifer has chosen Girl Rising.
www.girlrising.com

CONTENTS

Pyre: Wind As Hell Beast - 11
Afterlife: For Executioner Geoffrey Therage / Joan Of Arc Comes Back From The Dead - 12
On Methylphenidate A Breakdown Breakdown - 13
Dom Remy - 15
Jacques, The Manikin, And Joan - 16
Starlet - 17
P.J. Harvey Says She Is Going To Take Her Problems To The United Nations - 19
The Worst Thing Is That My Story Is Not The Story I Tell Myself Anymore - 20
Michael At Night, Catherine In The Day, Margaret In The Day - 22
Mixed Media Artist Jenny Holzer Speaks To Me From The 90s - 23
Land Surveyor - 25
Saiga - 27
A Simpler Time For Scientist Music - 29
Invocation: Joan Reads The Crowd - 31
Arrogant Grand Jetty - 32
Ants In The First Person - 33
She Came Out From Under The Bed #1 - 34
She Came Out From Under The Bed #2 - 35
She Came Out From Under The Bed #3 - 36
She Came Out From Under The Bed #4 - 37
She Came Out From Under The Bed #5 - 38
Cross The Brook - 39
Algebraic Seasick Monster - 40
Abscess: Joan Succumbs To Fever - 42

Lone Tree: Nature Communes In A Dream-Like Landscape - 43
The Cotton Of Her Blouse - 45
Siege Of Compiegne - 46
Lustmord - 48
Joan's Expedition Pauses At Four Points (Or, Team Building Exercise) - 49
A Rotary Phone - 50
Wings: Joan's Afterthought - 51
I Bite My Thumb At You Sir - 52
Two Friends - 53
Jenny Gives Me Orders - 54
Cross Dressers - 55
Joan's Cell - 57
Adieu, Neptune - 58
Field And Stream: Joan's Mise-En-Scene - 59
Shirt Collar - 60
Seven Ways To Disappear - 62
Pilgrimage - 63
Premonition Walk Part I - 65
Circles - 67
Time - 69
Dead Walk - 71
The Sleepwalker - 73
Premonition Walk Part II - 74
Industrial Walk - 75
Epilogue: Grackles - 77

FOR HELENIPA STEPHENS

PYRE: WIND AS HELL BEAST

The wind is a tease
prior to engulfment.

Joan is a dirty thought.

The transcriber's notes, read.
The guilty discover
death's gate,

like it was the future.

The spectrum of *other side*
splits into orange slices.
One: a battering ram of bones.
Two: a lost and found.

Remnants the plague left:

a tiny cosmos inside eyeballs
black rags rage
through an abnormal light vortex

Wooden throats (because saying the right thing sucks)
pierce prayers

Deliver messages through dead
carrier pigeons,
shadow puppets,
burnt tongues.

Joan dips a toe into the afterlife and she is glowing.

AFTERLIFE: FOR EXECUTIONER GEOFFROY THERAGE / JOAN OF ARC COMES BACK FROM THE DEAD

In her afterlife, Joan dreamt of opossums
squeezing under the scullery door.

Like revenge, she memorized cold soup recipes
lifted the lid too early, rescued molars to needle a necklace.

Mongrels don't stop thrashing about.
Burgundians lost their ladders
looking for sour men.

Wind blew religion into mouths like a herpes' sore.
Elevation should be effortless or you're not doing it right.

Burnt on three occasions, (Joan calls her murder an occasion,)
ashes clung to cat femur bones.
She crawls out of the Seine
depletes all sense back into the earth.

Fingers reach up through dandelions,
tickling worms to find him.

The clover spreads over orifices,
Creeping Charlie her minion,
the river bank bursts forth.

Strangled by his own hair shirt.
She kisses the ballooned face and gives pause.

A bowl of stars cupped in her palm is so beautiful.

ON METHYLPHENIDATE: A BREAKDOWN BREAKDOWN

    a paper doll   is ripped into bits by a plastic knife.
    a rain soaked cereal box, split open like lips, crumpled in the
        street
I wait for head lights. The time vault slams shut.

    time warps stop motion photography at fast intervals
    and the sound   the sound   the sound   is a freight train
    propelling down 5th avenue in the east and groaning up the
Cahone Pass in the west

    All of my brain   trains   start the slow slide back down the
mountain,   the rocks fall faster when you are high

    My insanity   is a broken glass sliver   in a goblet   that is
swallowed anyway

    meanwhile in this nursey rhyme   A dingo circles a tiny dog
    sees its own savageness

    a   white mask   that starts at,   no,   no, stares at, me
from outside glass, outside plastic, outside wood   would
insanity tied to wrists   and   ankles and face and what I am
trying to say is   is   parts the parts are made up

the walls blee_____they stop running down the clock.

Cornflakes on the side of a surgeon's mouth—like what else did
he rush through?
My insanity is octopus, shoe, stick, intestines, charred book,
exposed negatives

                                    I'm not fooling anyone

            fake wings   *you think you can get away*

from a most wanted poster in a video game from 1999
My insanity is a fan at a Prince concert of that same tour name
who cannot find her car
                alone in a sticky skin graph world

My insanity turns   my   torso into a bruised strawberry—
moldy, gray and fuzzy with:
                sweetness   it ripens

DOM REMY

Joan sees boots march over her torso.
The gowns and haircuts wanted to see for themselves.

Rants unfit for knowledge
lifted her into kinetic spasms of bone.

The tendons hung in tree branches
by her childhood church.

Nothing is wasted.
Joan reunites with all flesh and sings.

A split voice magnifies throughout the hills.
The help go home.

Earth is one big ash kingdom and a tibia.

Linen scraps, purity belts,
a scorched earth policy returns from England's gift shop.

The garrison commander came to her in a hazy trip.
She whispers to the beetles,
crawl into his ear.

Fingers pick thyme, feel for boot straps to tug, trip,
suffocate sour men in an inch of water.

Is it more unpleasant that way?
To hear life going on above the ear shell
to know that it will dissipate in suffocation slaughter?

How does pond scum taste?
Joan enjoys Sainthood.

JACQUES, THE MANIKIN, AND JOAN

Jacques cherished a modest means plane,
taxing and evading between
manikin and odd daughter.
Joan lifts her lips to sky ears twice a day.

Harder to hear the light,
she replaces ears with fly swarms.
The flies are angry the honey ran out.
Joan projects her anger onto bugs.

It's happened before:
the locusts' cacophonic legs
stumble about in chamber pots—
not enraged, just blind.

Too young to be a mother of a prophetess,
the manikin had to take it out on someone.
It created a blush
where there was none.

Joan starved herself
on Apostles in the fields
of Dom Remy just like
the English starved out the French.

Jacques fed the goat off his own plate.
Burgundians sharpened iron toys.
Taught how to be low
and stay that way,

Joan is a marmoset.
The unexpected kiss on her cheek,
a rivulet from Jacques' carving knife.
Not meant to use her looks.

STARLET

After Man Ray's 1926 film Emak Bakia, *Basque for "leave me alone."*

distant Marseilles domes
tell my future

a low heeled saddle shoe
is not immune to

entrapment bicycle
baguette variety

sparkle poodle show
400 blows at Epiphany

one cannot steal a
nailed down red carpet

style icon
for a funeral parlor

her poor bric-a-brac
scenario

pearls
bobbed hair

exposed lace shoulder
minuscule Grecian lip

your open eyes
painted on eyelids

bloom a towering
joke totem

throw shade
to the crowd

for a sad day coma

P.J. HARVEY SAYS SHE IS GOING TO TAKE HER PROBLEMS TO THE UNITED NATIONS

Who will kill the weeds in my back yard?
Who will stop my son from scratching kids at recess?
Will there be a panel discussion
on just the scratching
or just the weeds?
How many people will be on the panel?
Will I get to vet these people?
Will my mother-in-law be on the panel?
What if all the solutions are bad ones?
Does that make that word, "solution" not a solution?
But a "problem solution?" like a "problem play?"
What if I think the solutions are bad but the panel does not?
What if a lunch break comes too soon?
Like right when they are in the middle of some good solution talking?
What if a break comes too late and people's blood sugar drops?
Like really drops, hard, so that women in pearls pass out?
Like right when we are reaching some good compromise?
What if the men get angry because they are hungry?
What if I pass out from hunger?
What if there is no one to get home to my children because I have passed out?
What if I have been taken to a quiet office space to recover?
What if no solutions are reached because I am not in the room to
announce, *"yes, I agree to that."*
What if the solutions are reached because I am not there;
a proxy appoints herself to be my proxy and
she says, *"yes, I think Jennifer will agree to that."*
Or conversely, what if she says, *"no, Jennifer will never agree to any of this."*
What if I never agree?
What if I agree?
What if time stands still like in *The Twilight Zone*?
It's all pant suits and gavels now.

THE WORST THING IS THAT MY STORY IS NOT THE STORY I TELL MYSELF ANYMORE

For Jenny Holzer's exhibit "Lustmord," inspired in part by the Bosnian war, there was one card, printed in blood. The blood was donated by women volunteers, treated to kill contaminants, and then mixed with printing ink. Many men were outraged by this.

She wants you to touch it
with one fingertip
not just to *know* but to *feel*

a mashing teeth and
haircut strangulation

this horror show matinee
plays into the night

*what is inside you will come out
and this will make people want to
kill you*

Skin is a sealant
a silence we cannot hear
so much blood
our parts that
aren't supposed to
not want you, ever.

*to know is not enough
she wants you to feel it*

It's not enough to show
the victim's viewpoint but also:
perpetrator,
observer

enter the white space
the red space
the pink space
ending in no words: blackness

it is impure
to give what is inside
away, willingly

to explode
to burst
to heat up
to repeat

to not bandage
what one has done

MICHAEL AT NIGHT CATHERINE IN THE DAY MARGARET IN THE DAY

Saints can fucking exhaust you. The first time she was lifted by tree stumps she deplored life as a cut, dirty swan. Chasing voles, a husk shadow suffocated, bones protruded from his back. Being a suck-up, she didn't recognize his wounds. Slaying god's enemies brings on the gray. Slaughter the dark one, learn to avoid razors. *Drivethemout.* Do not speak because wings beat in time with mouth words. Refraction pulsed through his voice light. She was warm and elevated and grounded at the same time. His moth essence humming all the while. Catherine with her flowing hair and cumbersome gown that weighed in like silk and slime. Catherine held the flour down and burst words into a torso like feathers. Joan plucked the feathers out of her brain later, slowly, savoring the felt. Margaret the opposite, hardy and robust with vocal chords like lost calves and mourning mission bells, a blanket after shock therapy. The bells rung the world over. Tattered, but knowing something had changed, the girl cried, buried hands in the clay, practiced playing prisoner to mud.

MIXED MEDIA ARTIST JENNY HOLZER SPEAKS TO ME FROM THE 90s

Neon letter boxes infect Times Square
Holzer was obsessed with sex and war

I wish I could have seen your prophetic
billboards above strip clubs, Jenny:

Abuse of power comes as no surprise—
The contrast of pixelated dots

Hung over pasties in display windows, rat bodies
gleamed like slaps. Letters

looming over saliva splattered concrete.
Always blockade, always the same font,

(She would never use "Freestyle Script.")
She has no face.

Words hang in the air
two inches from ghost mouths.

Which came first—
the words or the mouth?

I am angry with you, Jenny.
All I wanted was to see

your pretty pink mouth
forming these words:

men cannot protect you anymore
In the Field museum

At that Biennale in Venice
At the Guggenheim.

I don't even know myself anymore
I thought I was bright

And elucidated brightness
when I read your words

I know I am still searching
for myself

Jenny posts
Your awful language is in the air by my head

I am on the corner of 42nd Street
and Broadway, pushing bodies like pencils,

no words in sight.

LAND SURVEYOR

On a different earth fire is magic.
Apple blossoms burned along
the Loire River Valley.

Sickly smells stumbled
drunk down a dark alley
and asked for it.

Devil hours later,
the trunk stood upright,
a husk of its former self.
Even the giving tree was grabby.

A bitchy forest
looked on from across the Meuse River,
trunks proud to avoid such a fate.

Three thousand scraps of armor
tattered banners, slain horses,
chafes of bread on the ground.

The only thing moving were the ants.
Tiny legs marched over
seared shoulders and thighs.

An elm, a watcher in the woods,
dead, but bearing witness, mourns parts.
Leaves, branches, and roots
search to be made whole again.

The elm looks for extensions of itself
floating seedlings. Ugly,
infant oaks shift their gaze earthbound,

wave twigs like bones, laugh in embarrassment.

Human parts share a beta moment,
cells fuse with rock.

Worms grow together, burn together.

SAIGA

Is it a mystery ungulate illness
or exploding chemicals from Russian test rockets?

No one knows. I look for you in the space
between the window screen and eternity.

So many particles I cannot name them
yet they add up to fusion. You and

your bulging antelope eyes roam the
Kazakhstan tundra. I have big eyes too

but I'm no wolf. Is it something in the
water? No human rides your antelope back –

maybe you long to feel weight,
to feel a torso crush you in the morning because

you want to feel necessary. We have all tired
from frequenting the same

beauty bars, your spongy
proboscis filtering out cold air and

dust, looking for a new Carpathian
Mountain to climb, like any Monday morning.

Your apathetic horns
spiral out of control. There

is no need to butcher you anymore
for eastern fertility rituals, pocket the horns,

leave the carcass to rot. The pathogens have seen
to that. Man exploded in population

while you imploded, even with
two thirds of calf births resulting in twins.

You cannot communicate
to the herd: *100% fatality.*

A SIMPLER TIME FOR SCIENTIST MUSIC

After Man Ray's 1926 film Emak Bakia, *Basque for "leave me alone."*

an eyebrow pencil control group
burns glass test tube aphasia

mirror spin string theory
rotate a deux grandes stomach rumbling

automobile winter cascade dream
it's this year's model

to bleed out using
leeches and a bowl

Like the sow toiling for truffles
her high heel kicks record

tonal angles
graph ding a ling dips

steals a quartet cacophony
social knees curtsy

above the appropriate
Victrola note hem length

banjo licks an isosceles arm
over pebbles and gray grass

ghost shins scrape dance
off the walls

tow corners into next week
knee joint angst plucks the pluckiest

violins   cannot keep up
see how dark the brow furrows

heaven's light tucked into
catastrophe pocket

walk to your sitting room
head live streaming regret

INVOCATION: JOAN READS THE CROWD

Some men desire sausage nailed to bark just for kicks.
Joan prefers sorting iron deposits to culinary remonstrations.

That's the true way to heathen caballus hearts.
Never downed a brandy—
talons took her liver in the after-life.
Like Chrissie Hynde, that brass in pocket left long ago.

Self-hacked curls are racy to ravens.
Joan would rather cut her fingers off then caress a waxen cheek

and it's all what time should we meet up after the war?

Primp the ocean with a poorly executed ax swing.
Mouths ravage sound waves.
It's her voice that mounts the men—
wingless mongrels with clumsy carbon footprints
I chose you for your pulsing qualities
Wikipedia left that part out.
Arm to stone to crushed ladder leg
Burning hair multitude and it's 1-0.

Joan thinks about hell and the
spears secret guts spill out.
Maniacal reds, virgin whites, pink pudding.
Grapefruit spoon in throat,

King Charles laughs a little boy laugh.

ARROGANT GRAND JETTY

After Man Ray's 1926 film Emak Bakia, *Basque for "leave me alone."*

brush fire flings cosmonauts ocean side
sea foam and short shorts calm

even the longest drawing room note,
our wiliest hour

cold carp flutters gills
those impatient hairdos

turntable dizzies and readies,
draws a bath zeitgeist

ancient runes rotate
forfeit and tremble

this Driver's Ed test
coerces us to

tremble, forfeit,
and rotate

any semblance of vision
lost on Capitol Hill

shapes multiply
deception buries hard hats

who destroyed your castle today?
the jumping man suit

the child's fists
sign this and triplicate

ANTS IN THE FIRST PERSON

A mob of mandibles.
Time is a construct,
burnt loaves in the fire.

I have left the 1400s
only to be brought to this maelstrom
of conceit and oversharing.

What land lubbers of dull shit crimes.
I slice myself with this blade
to show you what sharp is.

Fly through time zones
of dessert and stone age
how many burials must I see
before someone is sharp?

Up close I see epidermis like a red sea,
black stitches sew the infection in.
You cannot kill me
I am already dead from spit.

I have spread myself at midnight
and taken the plunge from the highest masthead.
Where is your spread?
What have you brought as offerings?

Crumbs of want,
I throw them to the eagles
who want more, rip lips off.

An arrow in my neck,
a knuckle in my skull.

My wings, internal intestines churning the eternity out.

SHE CAME OUT FROM UNDER THE BED #1

She came out from under the bed
rifled through drawers and drapes

a slipped format
next year's model

sounds of new build
sawdust

to fill earholes
chained malcontent

attempted robbery
escaped humming

to rouse a dark dawn

SHE CAME OUT FROM UNDER THE BED #2

She came out from under the bed
brought all legality thunder with her:
procurement contracts and readiness,
repurposed grenades, hag witch catastrophe

She does not know I command steeliness,
record my own short comings, rake leaves
from my hair and excavate throat dirt

Her face restyled with stainless steel guilt
and sun filled yesterdays the torso is an
all-night diner

I see the light now, streaming through pinholes

SHE CAME OUT FROM UNDER THE BED #3

She came out from under the bed reeking of salt, a particular stripped away-ness. Where are the dry counties? She began her riddle: *if I am moth filled and you are liquid...* Her seagull wings expanded, fish flopped out of her mouth and onto the mattress, seized in depleted oxygen. Fins gesticulated trying to grow fingers, my own palms cold, the scales blinking *hello, hello.*

SHE CAME OUT FROM UNDER THE BED #4

She came out from under the bed owning full vulture face

Don't worry, I only eat dead things

I cannot move, I signed. How do you know I am not dead?

Because you are talking to me

Maybe I invented you. I am always getting in my own way

That's right.

She started to peck at my upturned wrist,

splayed thigh

SHE CAME OUT FROM UNDER THE BED #5

She came out from under the bed
was all slow song and mother goose rhymes
All bonnet and hot tea and pink raspberries
Her tree bark skin was shaved smooth, the
birds' nests accumulating on the dresser

I raised these baby birds, I can do the same for you

She forced a worm down my throat

CROSS THE BROOK

Daffodils   bloomed   fell
from night   rain
her house panels of mist
I have always   been walking there
silent,   blinds drawn   rocks   breaking
morning fog
black dogs   in the clouds   along the ground
broken   moss   home
                                        She blends into the walls

She is jam on toast
brooch from 1945
cheeksosoft
gemstones on knuckles vary
            shawl hugs shoulders
Pulled   close in the back yard
The skirt   nylons,   nylons   nylons
                                  I never saw her in pants
        Not   one   single day

gravity's   sun room

pulls the notes from the air

fig bits strewn in the sink

The place where four oars paddle
no lake,

only the cotton of her blouse

ALGEBRAIC SEASICK MONSTER

After Man Ray's 1926 film Emak Bakia, *Basque for "leave me alone."*

variable D represents
        one mossy Argonaut
                phone a friend
                      sing for an unforeseen amount

of holding time hold music
        Figure eights dance
                seaweed is an unknown
                      as only strangers can

meet at an underwater photo shoot
        Venice beach caught a light sneeze
                the twine wraps around her ankles

two times two is the Charleston
        more complicated
                than dining for one at
                      sunset the mystery

heaves itself from low tide
        tips a shrunken hat to
                a prisoner of portraiture
                      her surf dims down to X

lists A to B
        no more ballroom dancing
                to follow the painted foot prints
                      the parlor awash in whiskey

breathe less
        but exhale more
                zero gets all the glory
                        vacuumed space celebrates

                                Freckles:
                                our map of diamonds

ABSCESS: JOAN SUCCUMBS TO FEVER

Playground gates open
welcomes underage arrows.
Capitulate on see-saws of swords,
oil barrels explode and
this joint is jumping.

A quiet sidelong glance:
all of the pretty ones she never gave birth.
A tiny warmth,
suckling animal attached to
sick skin.

Leading all pretend children to slaughter
sliced spam sandwiches.
Deliver higher light by carrier pigeon,
this isn't story hour.

The infection takes hold.
Screams about being "selfish" so the neighbors hear.
A snake and a raven
complete the hallucination.

Which one to sacrifice?
Flip a coin and break a bone.
Look for eyes to peck out.
Select eyes or ears to go.
Which do you need less.

LONE TREE: NATURE COMMUNES IN A DREAM-LIKE LANDSCAPE

Never picture ready, Joan of Arc is also illiterate. A catnap under a weeping willow and branches pen the future on themselves: papyrus was cheap in 1430.

The Elm as dark sky serpent.
The Elm as ink challenged octopus
clutching eight styluses.

Deciduous beasts cheated all of history's
Haikus. Keeping secrets
behind initialed trunks.

Huge dinner plate
leaves are refracted elbows.
Stroke a soft shoulder.

Joan stirs,
hates a gentle breeze.
Knowing one is a good fit for a cause
is different than swimming with poisonous tree frogs.

French optimism floods the springs not with macaroons,
but mercury laden sewer water.

Now the conqueror of snow-capped mountains, tremors.
Who is she kidding? The beetles spawn, flip over on their backs,
wave six legs in the air: a friendly gesture goes unnoticed.

This vaudeville act ended hours ago.
Play this tea party out.

Flesh and brain cannot comprehend
such a placid Monet mise-en-scene.
Slice it with a butcher knife and it is a mere fragment,

no music to entice punctured ear drums,
no teeth and tongue parting
to sing along the Seine.

An embrace from the inside is all anyone wants.
Like females, lava has a love hate relationship with rules.

THE COTTON OF HER BLOUSE

waivers
against staff paper   torso paper dart shadow

perfect rectangular bench
drifted   night   mosquito   circumference hum

weighted   crab grass breaths
sweetest notes   exit porch door

E major   G minor   C major chords
lowest gravitas utilizes B flat

letters plunk   disappear into dusty corners
Repeat

repeat
crescendo

A staccato   that little death
Mezzo piano   unfolds   pulls a melancholy tide

it is here
no, here

an instrument   knocks,   hammers fall,   strum
under ghost light

ivory old time heat
succumbs to the pedal

a fox hides in blackberries

SIEGE OF COMPIEGNE

Even rocks betray you.
Chucked from above,
split over silver fish
helmets scampering
up the wall.

Not burned, stuck in the walls,
keystones have nothing else to look at.
They smirk at dead bodies.
When the talisman

reads Joan's transcribers notes
it is already too late.
The last group to leave the bar,
the battlefield leftovers,

eyes speak *Guillaume de Flavy*: traitor.
His party trick of locking
gates behind everyone
flayed facial skin.

Joan's last act
in the Hundred Years War
was meeting dirt with her face.
Butcher men, sour men,

like to pull things off of other things.
Once, a blood orange spectrum
of battering rams against torsos
and teeth assaulted dusk's skyline.

Now the end.
Joan found a higher,
abnormal light,
put it in her pocket.

She knows her molecules will burst at a million degrees.
Enemy thighs squat, break bread over beef stock.
Crush the crusts into juice.
God is too small.

LUSTMORD

Jenny says all wars start as a secret
She inks models' skin with letters, sentences
My eyes are sore from moving against your palm
Some phrases carry a hint of threat
Of women squatting
Of being taken
She makes me want to
slam the book shut
take a shower, get a haircut.
Self-awareness can be crippling
The information age blew our
brains open to stay
Terrorists stream live video,
machete all the words
In the desert it takes
longer to find a dictionary
longer still to locate
synapse centers
palm a sound,
hold it in your throat
swish it around
claim one last guttural noose
War is a purification rite
There are no emoticons
in dictatorships, Jenny
Pandas eating jellybeans,
cherry cola bottle,
kitty holding heart,
to ease all of that
genocide
The air turns smelly
A dead rat trapped under the fridge word
A rotten chicken breast word
A cacophonic fly swarm word
A dog rolling in its own vomit word
You are trapped in these words so you will explode

JOAN'S EXPEDITION PAUSES AT FOUR POINTS (OR, TEAM BUILDING EXERCISE)

I didn't say it was your fault that brought us here you three-legged cur. I hit send ages ago. All messages waste away through severed hands and serpent tongues. Maybe my essence can send a message. Your last gasp in this swamp caused interference with the light. Four points was a shitty meeting place anyway. Dropped off at rosy-assed dawn to meet reinforcements, now we've lost our guide because he was run through. Parents are probably dead. No one asks to travel back in time. It just happens when reading the phone book at midnight. This rock schism sheared part of Henri's scalp off and you don't hear him bitching about his dead pony. Alan has poison sumac all over his face from an infected feline hidden in his gunny sack. We all have problems. His word still must be killed over and over and the redundancy files lost in the shredding machine hidden in the barn of some commoner five thousand times over. How many times can I kill the same men and myself? All for a mere message? Let's call this wasteland a day. Bake some cookies and go to the pool.

A ROTARY PHONE

After Man Ray's 1926 film Emak Bakia, Basque for *"leave me alone."*

parlay brown eye
time travel into

white teeth
flicker the commercial

erase wire electrocution
your face is every

forsythia every bee
stung lip

annual rates drop
manual dial tones forsake

the silent muse slicks sly
cheeks burst like crystal

goblets land
a new time share

the waves swallow
punctuation

WINGS: JOAN'S AFTERTHOUGHT

Obsolete creatures are supposed
to be terrifying.

She always hears the wings behind her.
The big fat softness
flirts with her
shoulder blades,
eyeing a flat back.
I'd rather be camping

blinks the voicemail message
behind third eye enlightenment
Post-it notes
litter the battlefield
Pepper dandelions with
shades of cowardice.

Silversmiths, bakers, and
candlestick makers leave the nursery
rhyme just in time to
betray her.
She pelts an asterisk
at the English dictionary.

I dare you,
call me devil
Still, she cries
at all of the little feet.

I BITE MY THUMB AT YOU SIR

After Man Ray's 1926 film Emak Bakia, *Basque for "leave me alone."*

this box
is a
hat box
which holds
a man's
hat but
he signs
away his
hat box
for one
wooden nickel
one light
bulb one
pen, one
watch, and
one last
grasp at
his hat
which is
the sum
of his
human
costume

TWO FRIENDS

Intimacy exists in learning how to write. Chemical reactions between fingers and quill burst like neon petunias. A precious childhood snow globe scene: time times vulnerability times trust equals: voice. A voice is a reassuring shadow, constantly surrendering to vibrations lapping behind you, a joy known as__(insert best remembered joy here)_____. The functional magnetic resonance imaging displays rainbow lines during a good laugh. Soldiers believe in songs like twenty North stars. All tourists enjoy pinning a journey's end. Whole like a muddy Robin's nest, or an ear shell. Torso grown arms are not familiar with softness. Think the darkness is winning, like sarcasm is not really a style of joking, meteors whine through the wind like a muffler in the suburbs. But this was France. Everyone drives a scooter. Through a burnt vineyard, darkly. An open door to Robert de Baudricourt: who provided armor and a horse. Gifts are to keep ones with you. To fall and the other lifts. When mouths are open, the corners of sunset hide on the earth and don't set. When friendship goes bad it is moldy bread, a hostage turned terrorist in a closet.

JENNY GIVES ME ORDERS

Remember to react

Protect me from what I want

Claim unauthorized space

Instructions
fill trees with fruit.
I gladly photosynthesize,
Lift my soft palette
but find it cumbersome.
Freedom to spread
lips together, teeth apart
so we choke
on our own preferred travel
advertisements.
The blue light special
extinct along with print.
What is easy evolution?
Take a perception vacation.
Our tongues cannot move
as fast as hummingbird wings.
We relinquish
space between the
dark age
the Imax age
the Twitter feeds.
Drones deliver a soft look.
I couldn't buy a soft look
if it hit me with a frying pan.

CROSS DRESSERS

At this tea party of benches and Bibles,
the lecturer is part drone, all queen bee.

All of the bigwigs wear wigs. They
need more hair to think.

Posturing as females,
the powdered procure statements.

The Statements sound like questions.
The questions spit syllables like a furtive glance.

Like a good Democrat,
Joan attempts a reach across the aisle
but she never learned furtiveness.

A grandiose evening filmed for CNN or Soul Train,
all the interesting bits are off camera.

It's all *"take my pocket square,"* and *"Comb out that nest."*
The robed ones might as well model maxi dresses.

They in drag, She in garb.
Statues sit and stare at each other through stained glass and
vaulted ceilings.

Go on, tell your tea party story how I came from underground
I will recap how they came from the sky.

Our ears will foster care sounds of treason and devil.
You do the ranting. I will do the pouring.

At the end of month's end, whispers of pyres,
of throwing a cat in for the ride, I will succumb.

All because I would rather be right than apologize.
All that's missing are knuckle rings and a boom box.

JOAN'S CELL

What an after school special.
The word *peasant* might as well have been spray painted red across the chamber,

dripping with urban set design.
This wasn't the Scarlett Letter.

Joan's wool tunic clings to her like a cheap
Halloween costume, smells different in the rain.

The nuns strive to keep her sane with conversation
about how pretty the light is.

Men in disguise, visit, want to persuade,
fake pleasantries, like with any sex worker in boys clothes.

What a cliché. The nuns examine her every night.

What is underneath? That turns the robes on as well. Though fingers find her human, the white hoods speak as if they were talking about an animal. *She shows intelligence* (sow) *very eloquent* (horse) I understand! *Amazing robustness, yet a gentle heart* (cow) *she carries a heavy load* (ass.) Still, what a bitch.

ADIEU, NEPTUNE

After Man Ray's 1926 film Emak Bakia, *Basque for "leave me alone."*

water a hair shirt
see what grows

guilt buttons
rage sleeve

your own importance
cannot stand still

a constant reminder
you kissed first

my skirt has the flu
scalpel headache layers

with hot and cold compresses
gentle moth wings beat

the Ferris
wheel of doubt

whirling so fast
skinny ants legs

swing in time to the
Music of Chance

laughter too light
propagates outer space

sound bubbles
wishing away eyelashes

FIELD AND STREAM: JOAN'S MISE-EN-SCENE

She was remembering that she was remembering…

Stallions writhed in the
Sully-sur-Loire muck
Manes tangled up amongst
legs and soap opera sighs
Sunken curvatures, broken
backs backed into themselves

Joan pulls an arrow
out of her own neck
eats grub infested porridge
covers her face in mud
Hundreds of years later

The overly footnoted painting
By Ingres
Joan of Arc at the Coronation of Charles VII
revered by thousands
Hangs in the Louvre
Glows in red and silver

Commissions made:
Give her long hair
Put her in a dress

SHIRT COLLAR

After Man Ray's 1926 film Emak Bakia, Basque for "leave me alone."

a trapped swan is
crumpled Kleenex

don't you see it's
crisp wings

begging to flee
a sunburnt neck?

Stubble the little people
razor apathy

flying is an unforeseen
frozen

fingertip
pushed into

a modern art
phonograph

dreaming of suit jackets
to tuck itself in at night

faster and faster
flying poison dart

circus of cleanliness
sepia infused

tea manikin dust

this attire is gauche

a piano writes letters
to formal wear

light a candle
grow some malice

in a petri dish

SEVEN WAYS TO DISAPPEAR:

1. Invite the trees into your home and let the branches and leaves overtake you. Soon blossoms will grow from the stems between your nose and chin: not two lips but tulips.

2. Throw a party and invite one hundred people. When the party is in full swing, offer to go out for ice even if no one asked for any, and hit the interstate. Keep driving. No one will miss you until maybe the day after, even if you are in a relationship. Relationships are hard.

3. Find a dense wood by your home and go for a run. Don't tell anyone. Keep walking and hitch a ride from some fishermen. Fishermen like to mind their own business.

4. Befriend oceanographers and David Blaine and get them to make you a glass case that can exist underwater. Move into this glass case and wave at sea turtles.

5. Offer to take someone to the airport. Then once you see them off, go work at the Food court. Food courts exist in their own realm and time continuum.

6. Draw a map that has no points from A to B, only D's, F's, and M's. All the semi-middle, and middle points. Scatter colons about the middle of the map: to be contined.

7. Don't look at all of your belongings. They will remind you where you got them and you will think of your life's story and the origins of that story, instead of the here and now of that story which is: you want to disappear.

PILGRIMAGE

Lips to Saint Joan's ears,
brown hoods cup water
in their tiny hands,
scavenging for bits of bone in the Seine.

A blacksmith remembers her:
Fragile and lemur-like,
raked over the coals
three times to
wring the witch out.

Psalm pages hang in the branches
Of the weeping willows,
heavy with the softness of girl's skin.
Branches miss their little doll
with high cheek bones.

Like Cinderella's birds
Who knew too much
Clothing scraps woven into
nests for remembrance near
the family farm.

The proverbial sword struck
down the tiniest shape;
everyone wants to harm little girls.
Crowns not up to contemplating
the cosmos, acquiesce throughout eternity.

The healing is measured.
Firstonebreath.
Thenasecond.

Then a year has gone by.
measured by guest book signatures.

Creeping in from forests,
forms conjoin to assemble
one gargantuan black robed priest.
The townspeople sweep,
chant, light candles,

cradle pieces of warmth,
this one I will protect, that one, lost.

PREMONITION WALK PART I

Inspired by images from *The Nuremberg Chronicle* (1493)
natural phenomena, unnatural births, and birthmarks as omens.

There was only half a torso
in the middle of the highway:
the mound of hair and pink parts unidentifiable,
one automatically thinks: a bad omen.

If the birthmarks weren't already on my babies'
thighs…

no, that's not right, only one twin has a mark

begging the question, where is the mark of the
other?

If he was not marked coming into this world
will he be taken early, was he not meant to be here.

The light brown moth wings that imprint
my upper thigh
span one son's leg as well,

but not the other.

Medical texts say it's due to the ways
fetuses move in the womb, to skin pigmentation

Or birthmarks foretell:
if you were shot in a passed life
if you will drown in the future
if you looked at fire too long
if the mother is vengeful

if the mother is lustful
if an angel kissed you
if a devil inhabits your body
if you once were a snake

I help my son get dressed everyday
I always look for a mark.

CIRCLES

After Man Ray's 1926 film Emak Bakia, Basque *for "leave me alone."*

are not hard headed
aloof hexagons

your pale oval face
collides into daffodils
no smelling salts needed

just curve lower backs into
a chaise lounge
cat eye glasses fog up

tiny doll
teeth grimace

snap fingers for
biscuits and tea, roll the dice
to misdirect thighs

signage points this way to
the last school dance

that way to the first
polar bear club

minus the fur and paws
a thought bursts

into firecracker detritus
the exact moment

you ask a question about
God wearing a black

suit jacket with
white pin stripes

because he knows
how to dress for a funeral

or a small struggle under the soil

TIME

Does time pass differently in the basement when one is afraid to go down there? Fear time moves faster than non-fear time. This is called

dark time. Sometimes there is no time continuum and one is out of time/ like the REM song or Huey Lewis and the News proclaim to get back in time. Is back in time

hidden time? superficial time? lost time? stolen time? mismanaged time? loving time? time to get it on?

time to get down to business? time to squander? time to eat one's cares away? time to rock around the clock?

time to waste? time to savor? time to bottle? Thyme time? time to count down the final countdown? Time to hold on to—

like a Precious Moments statue that was just meant to be smashed at a garage sale? I mean their eyes are so creepy and they have adult facial structures like they've already seen too much of the time they were given

There is Somewhere in Time, the movie with Jane Seymour and Christopher Reeves before his paralyzing time and it was his time to shine.

Now it's time to replace with etc, time to lie, time to lay down, time to lie again, time to give thanks, time to win, time to lose,

time to be the best and time to be the worst before one is hung in A Tale of Two Cities. There is the passage of time and even now, in this moment, some of us still do not have the correct calendar up where all the weeks and days are mismatched but you can't stop looking at it, trying to find the right time to be up to date.

DEAD WALK

Artist Jenny Holzer created a memorial in Hauptplatz, Austria fifty years after the end of World War II.

rectangular white stones
direct the
ghost girl
along the garden path

her boots leave
ash foot prints
black tulips stand
irreverent, upright

Who lived in the woods

we are just as see through
as you the flowers
mock the girl
in the breeze

Her bobbed hair
stringy, gray before
her time

Who ran to the river

one sign of benign script
take a towel and bar of soap

come and slash
my neck is
more honest

a charade of stainless steel
shower heads a
secret welcomes to feel
death

Who died looking

what is born in you
will come out
and this makes
people want to kill
you

the tulips drop
petals
at the ghost girl's
feet which skip back
into the lake

The beam of light
shoots into the night sky.
It is gone by dawn.

Whose thoughts are missing

THE SLEEPWALKER

After artist Lilli Carré

She always moved while sleeping:
along sidewalks, through the woods.

Leapt from rock to rock
bruised and cut up.

She always
ended up in the water.

It was the seaweed hanging from
her chin that woke her.

Herbal tea
daytime exercise
Russian novels:

it was all an attempt to get a
good night's sleep.

What are you looking for? People would ask her
during the day

Where do you go?

In search of something to hold me down

PREMONITION WALK PART II

In *The Nuremberg Chronicle* (1493)
There are Illustrations of Rainbows

And also:
blood exploding from the sky
two headed cherubs
four armed forest spirits

The charcoal drawing of the sun
drenched field is
serene and lovely

while the four legged cherub is an oddity:
he cannot move from the river bank

He drinks all the water he wants
but he does not know how to stand up

Our gods are two legged
and created in the image of man

we leave the monsters in the fairy tales
where they belong

a meager coping mechanism
never beginning to imagine

INDUSTRIAL WALK

I want to creep and burst
into a warm fog bruise
cover synapses and explode
off my mega pound rocks

                Like drooling dogs they drip
                and people don't know
                they are supposed to clean up
                their own messes

Maybe the sun will come out
tomorrow on the internet
and burn this sink hole life
left to ponder reflexology maps

                I hear the echoes, feel the feels
                every two hours,
                tamp me with indifference.
                Trainers, sandals, heels

hurt me

I feel luxurious for a second

feeling

them up

             I hold
          a grounding ground,
       a one way relationship—
          like with a therapist

No one wants to give themselves

to my grit
not *feeling* John Berger's *Ways of Seeing*
and his grubby hands

I am a self-help village
This platform would smother others
The thought is revealed in the step
safety dance safety camp

                    I resulted from one rotation
                    of gray matter churn,
                    laid down in water bed softness
                    then hardness everywhere

It was the only way to suffocate
sound

              Still, there might be an open rivulet

EPILOGUE: GRACKLES

Roberto raven circles the battlefield, waits for the logs and squares to stop shaking and gurgling. Opposite of Quick Care, the beaks seek grossness, go to the quiet ones first. Little silver boxes squirm in the grass. Two argue in the sky *If someone is dead, do you say "I love" or "I loved."*

Birds are just addicts who come to any gathering for the free coffee. The buzzing molecules won't stop mowing science down. New diagrams of buzzards break open encyclopedias. No one has any ears to hear the panting and murdered ecology. Put your energy into this field project management. Weed, mow, pluck, fertilize. Goats are good at bloodletting. Harvest the forearms and flies. You can tell how old something is by the smell.

Roberto, the only feathered Italian in France at the time, is outnumbered by the xenophobic blackbirds. Christopher chipmunk's only interest is nuts. Roberto is pissed and finds his voice again in the sky: message my wing beats in screams and piercing darkness through round orbital messages in a bottle. Christopher and Roberto are too scary to be illustrated properly. Real life never stops pulsing long enough for a proper water color. Roberto refuses to blind the corpses. A prisoner in another camp looks east, the morning bells ring. Armor a memory like the ocean.

And it's over a thousand years later and we are back on the banks of the Seine, opening a bottle of wine with a cork screw, loosening hiking boots. Telling each other about our small steps every fucking day.

ABOUT JENNIFER MACBAIN-STEPHENS

Jennifer MacBain-Stephens is also the author of the full length collection *Your Best Asset is a White Lace Dress* (Yellow Chair Press, 2016,) as well as eight chapbooks. Her chapbook *Dixit: Every Picture Tells a Story, or The Wrong Items*, is forthcoming from White Knuckle Press in 2017 and *She Came Out From Under the Bed: Poems Inspired by the Films of Guillermo del Toro* is forthcoming from Dancing Girl Press. Recent work can be seen at Lime Hawk, The Chiron Review, Jet Fuel, glittermob, concis, decomp, and Inter/rupture.

https://jennifermacbainstephens.wordpress.com